THE SPIDER'S PET

Diania Dboss
The Spider's Pet

Published by Spines
ISBN: 979-8-89950-836-3

Spines

THE SPIDER'S PET

DIANIA DBOSS

CONTENTS

CHAPTER 1

THE CRACK IN THE WEB

"AAAAHHGGGG!!! I FREAKING HATE YOU!"

The words exploded out of me before I even knew I was going to say them.

Mom's face recoiled like I'd slapped her across the soul. Her mouth hung open, torn between slapping me back or just dissolving into tears. Her dark eyes, filled with something sharp and sad, cut into me deeper than any lecture ever could. I hated that look. It made me feel... gross. Like a villain and a victim all at once. I didn't want to be either.

But I didn't wait to figure out which one I was.

I spun on my heel and stormed down the hallway. That's when it happened. My left foot decided to betray me and go on a solo mission under that stupid, lumpy rug that MOTHER *refuses* to throw away. I stumbled hard, caught myself, and yanked at the thing with rage boiling in my chest.

Instead of pulling it up, I redirected that fury to the bathroom door. Slammed it. Locked it. Let the walls catch the echo of my scream.

"I HATE IT HERE!"

I roared it like a stadium chant, loud enough to crack the air, not just the door.

The smell of warm vanilla bean-buttercream wax melts, Mom's obsession, poured into my nose. I gagged on it. Why the heck would you use vanilla in a bathroom? Isn't that a kitchen thing or something? Bruh!!!! My mom is so weird.

My chest heaved, lungs burning like a dragon's. Still, the silence that followed was worse than the yelling. It pressed down on me, too still, too loud in its quiet.

I picked at one of the many scabs on my wrist. I was self-harming again, just wanting to release the pain, but I couldn't hold it in anymore; my fist rose like it had a mind of its own and met the mirror.

Glass cracked like lightning, but it didn't shatter. It just… stayed. Broken and somehow still standing, like me.

I whispered through smoke and grit:

"I hate it here."

Hi. My name's Skylark.

Yeah. That's my real name. My *government name,* if you can believe it.

You are...? Oh! Cool. Whatever!

So, here's the deal: my mom named me after a bird. A *freaking bird*! Or maybe the song, or some poem no one remembers. She said I came out screaming, arms flailing like I was trying to fly. Cute, right?

She told me that story so many times it makes me want to puke. Said I was born to soar, to sing, blah blah blah. But I think "Skylark" sounds like the name of someone fragile, gentle, full of hope. That's not me. Not anymore. I feel more like a Ravyn. Or a Lilith. Something dark. Unreachable. Misunderstood.

And when I turn eighteen?

Yeah. I'm changing it. Just watch me.

Oh, one more thing you should know:

Although I have a bold exterior, I'm *deathly* afraid of spiders.

Don't laugh.

I don't mean "Ew, gross!" afraid, I mean full-body freeze, heartbeat-in-my-throat, shadow-in-my-brain kind of afraid. Arachnophobic, clinically and soul-deep.

I saw it before I knew I saw it. Just a flicker. A shadow skating across the bathroom wall.

My breath caught. My body reacted before my mind even processed it.

It wasn't big. But it didn't have to be.

Its legs moved too smooth, too confident, like it *knew* it was wrong and liked it. It emerged out of the cracked mirror and sat just above it, perfectly still. Its tiny body seemed to pulse, breathing, or maybe just *watching*. I know, I know, spiders don't *watch* people. But this one did. It watched *me*.

I couldn't scream. Couldn't even blink. My brain knew it was just a spider, but my body? My body thought it was death in eight-legged form. The air thinned. My thoughts tangled. My chest locked up.

It didn't move.

It didn't have to.

It turned the bathroom into a prison, the silence into a scream.

And then...

I must've blacked out. Yet, I don't remember falling. I barely remember what day it was. Time's been... slippery lately. Long, gray days blending into each other like watercolors left in the rain.

But when I opened my eyes... I wasn't in the bathroom anymore.

The ceiling above me shimmered with webs, glistening silver and glowing like thread made of moonlight. The air was thick and sticky, like breathing through silk.

I couldn't move.

My wrists were wrapped. Bound, not tight, but held

together in place.

I was hanging. Suspended. Trapped.

Not metaphorically. Literally.

I kicked. I twisted. The gluey silk held me together. The more I fought, the more it gripped.

Then something moved in the dark.

Slow. Deliberate.

Eight legs slid into view. Then the body, huge, black, *wrong*. Not just big. Wrong in that uncanny way, like it wasn't really an animal, but something... *else*.

It didn't just crawl.

It *approached.*

Then its face began to shift.

It was faceless at first. A dark void. But then a shape pushed through. A grin. A cruel, too-familiar grin.

Mom's smile.

The one she used to wear when she was pretending everything was fine.

"Hello, Skylark," it said in her voice, except... not. It was her voice braided with every painful thing I'd ever heard or thought about myself.

I couldn't speak.

"What… what is this?" I managed to whisper.

It leaned closer. "This is home now. I found you when you fell. When no one else noticed. You wanted to disappear, didn't you?"

"No," I breathed. "I was just… tired." I thought this

had to be a dream cause I'm talking to a freaking spider with a weird ass face.

"But tired becomes still. And still becomes mine."

Its eyes, my mother's eyes. Hundreds of them blinked at me. Black as obsidian. Cold as nothing.

"You were unraveling," it purred. "I only finished the job."

I felt like throwing up. It wasn't just a spider, it was my depression. My fear. My guilt. My every unspoken scream.

"What do you want from me?!"

It smiled even wider. "To keep you. To wrap you tight so nothing hurts anymore. No pain. No struggle. Just peace... forever." Well, that's creepy, I thought.

It sounded like a lie.

I looked around. Every thread of the web pulsed with something: anger, grief, regret. Each strand was *mine*. I had built this cage, thread by thread, without knowing.

This wasn't a prison.

It was a mirror.

And I had helped make it.

"No," I said, louder this time. "This isn't peace. It's a coffin."

The spider shrank back. "Ungrateful little thing."

Something woke in me. Something small, but solid. The tiniest ember of fight, of *me*.

I stopped struggling. I started focusing. On my truth. My pain. The part of me that *wanted* to live, even if I didn't know how.

"I'm not yours," I said. "I'm mine."

The web trembled. Threads snapped, one by one.

The spider shrieked, not with sound, but with memory. My father's rage. My friends' betrayal. The echo of silence when I needed someone most.

The badass in me screamed back.

And the world shattered, I slipped into the darkness again....

CHAPTER 2
THREADED SILENCE

I woke up again, wrapped in a breath I didn't take.

Everything shimmered. Overhead, the ceiling pulsed softly like it was alive, woven from silk so fine it could have been spun from stars. My arms were pinned to my sides. My legs wouldn't move. I wasn't lying down. I was *hanging*. Suspended midair swaddled tight like some kind of broken puppet.

I tried to scream, but all that came out was a dry, shallow gasp. The air felt thick, like breathing through cotton soaked in honey. Each inhale scratched at my throat. Panic came on hard and fast, rising through my chest like a tide I couldn't swim against.

And then I saw her-*it*-or whatever this thing was that stole my mom's face.

It was still. Waiting. Watching.

Perched just across from me, massive, gleaming, black with joints like jagged steel and eyes like wet stones. Eight of them-*eight of my mom's eyes*-reflecting the glow of the web.

Its gaze wasn't the mindless twitch of a bug. It *saw* me.

It looked at me like it understood. Like it was thinking. Studying. Judging.

It was like an alien, or a mythical creature. Almost... human.

My blood turned cold. I couldn't tear my eyes away. Something about it, about the way it sat there, unbothered, so perfectly still, it made my skin crawl from the inside out. This wasn't an animal. This was something else. Something *old.* Something that had been waiting for me to fall for a very long time.

Was it...

Did I...

My mind drifted to my life just moments before. Was I in a different world, permanently?

Had I finally crossed over into that weird in-between space between a meltdown and madness?

I remembered the way the bathroom door shook behind me. The look on Mom's face, like I'd just shattered her into glass. Again.

Then it all came flooding in.

The fight I had at school with Layla because she

posted that "funny" TikTok of me stimming in class. The failed math quiz. The way Mr. Lumsden sighed and muttered, *"You'd do so much better if you just applied yourself."*

Well, I've got news for you, buddy! I *was* applying myself. I was just trying to breathe.

Trying to look normal when your brain is going 150 mph in a 30 zone is exhausting. Trying not to cry when someone says, "You're too dramatic." Trying to remember to take your meds on time. Trying not to forget my backpack, my homework, my locker combo,

my worth.

I think that's the part no one really gets. It's not the "hyper" part. It's not the grades or the yelling or the scars they think are for attention. It's the part where you *try so hard* to be okay, and you still end up here.

Strung up in your own mess. Watched by the thing you fear most: *your own mind made monstrous.*

The spider didn't blink. It didn't speak. But it didn't have to.

It was me. Twisted.

Perhaps it was a part of me that grew in the dark when no one was looking. A flicker of motion. The spider tilted its head, if spiders even *have* heads. It moved one spindly leg forward like it was testing the air. Like it was *curious.*

"Why are you always running?" a voice echoed.

It wasn't out loud. It was inside me. Or under me. Or inside the threads.

"I'm not," I whispered. But the silk around my chest tightened slightly, like it knew I was lying.

I saw flashes, like lightning strikes of my life flickering without permission.

Me, age six, hiding under a table while my babysitter searched for me.

Me, nine, in the school nurse's office with a stomachache that wouldn't quit because I kept reliving what my babysitter did to me.

Me, eleven, being called to the principal's office because I was caught vaping in the bathroom.

Impulsive. Moody. Defiant. Too sensitive.

Every word ever pinned to me echoed now, like they were part of the web.

"I'm not broken," I said again, louder this time. My voice cracked.

The spider rose slightly, swaying with its massive body, silk threads humming with its movement.

"You wanted to disappear," it said. This time, the voice came through the air, wrapping itself around me like a lullaby dipped in poison. "You said so. In the bathroom. In the quiet."

I shook my head, but it felt weak. Shaky.

"That was just, just a thought. A tired thought."

"Thoughts are seeds," it whispered. "And you watered this one with silence. I just harvested it."

No. No, no, no.

I clenched my fists or tried to. The silk pulsed against me. But inside, something fought back.

A spark. Small, but there. The same spark that made me kick my feet when I was born. The one that got me in trouble and out of trouble. The one that made my heart say *not yet* even when my mind said *I give up.*

My name is Skylark. Birds don't belong in webs.

And I wasn't going to stay.

CHAPTER 3

WHEN THE MIND UNRAVELS

The threads creaked.

Not like a rope, but like memories. Twisting. Tensing. It moved in closer, and I panicked and did what I did best. I blacked out. When I came to, this freaking spider had the web around my neck. It tugged on the web which made me move forward, I tried to resist. This is stupid, I complained.

It glided forward then came to an abrupt stop which made me lose my balance. It laughed the most maniacal laugh. Watching. Waiting.

I blinked, and the glow of the web flickered.

Suddenly, I was ten again.

Sitting in the school hallway with my back to the wall, knees up, arms crossed so tight I felt like I could snap my own bones. My ears rang with the echoes of someone, some teacher, calling my name, but I couldn't respond. My head was too full. Too fast. Like a network error.

The web pulsed like a heartbeat around my neck. Then suddenly, it flew me into the air and flipped me over. I was hanging like a bat. I hung there, my arms limp, my body swaying gently in the still, thick air. Below me, the strands curved downward into the shadows, stretching into endless darkness. I couldn't see the floor. I wasn't even sure there *was* a floor anymore.

The spider, my spider, because that's what my brain wanted to call it, climbed on a single silk thread. Effortless. Elegant. Horrifying. Its eight legs touched the threads like a musician tuning strings. Its many eyes studied me with quiet intensity.

"You don't have to keep struggling," it said, in my mother's voice again, but softer this time. Sweeter. Like the fake calm she tried to use when she wanted me to take my meds without a scene. And you talk too much, I responded. With that smart mouth of yours, I should keep you here and make you my pet.

Your Pet! What the heck! I yelled in disbelief. My voice now dry and shaky.

"You *could* be," it whispered.

Something cold slid across my collarbone. I looked down, barely able to move my neck, and saw a thin, glowing thread winding itself around my throat. It wasn't choking me. Not yet. It was delicate. Like a leash. Or a collar.

"See?" the spider said. "Isn't that better?"

I felt sick. The thread shimmered like starlight, but it hummed with something darker. Powerless. Soft. Pretty. *Tamed.*

"You don't want to fight anymore," it cooed. "You're tired. You've always been tired."

And then, like a curtain being yanked open, the web around me fell away into color, and I was *somewhere else entirely.*

A hallway. My old school.

Fluorescent lights buzzed overhead. Lockers slammed shut like doors to tiny prisons. The noise was deafening. My backpack was open again, books spilling everywhere. Someone was laughing. Someone else was walking right through me like I wasn't even there.

My feet couldn't move.

Then I saw myself.

Twelve years old. Skinny. Wobbly knees. Eyes like a startled rabbit's.

I watched myself stare down a teacher who was holding up my crumpled math quiz like a used napkin. Big red X's covered every inch. Across the top, in angry sharpie: *"Did you even TRY?"*

I knew that face. That look of trying not to cry in

public. Trying to hold everything together with spit and sarcasm.

"You always broke too easily," the spider said, its voice echoing through the hallway.

Suddenly, the scene melted, colors dripped away like wax, and I was on the kitchen floor at age fourteen, curled up with my hoodie over my head, Mom shouting from the doorway: *"What is WRONG with you?"*

Then, in a counselor's office, legs bouncing, fingers tapping, eyes darting everywhere, while some woman with a soft voice and soft clothes said, *"Maybe we need to adjust your dosage."*

Then: a hospital bed. Bright lights. Beeping machines. A nurse pressing a warm hand to my arm, like I was already fading.

My chest ached.

The web re-formed around me, slow and sticky. And the spider leaned in close enough that I could smell it, not like an insect, but like something metallic and deep. Old wood. Damp stone. Forgotten places.

"You don't belong in their world," it murmured. "You never did. But you *belong* here. With me. I'll take care of you. No more masks. No more failure. Just silence. Just rest."

The collar pulled gently.

A tug.

Not hard. Just enough to get me on the ground and make me feel like following.

Good girl, the voice inside the silk whispered.

Something in me started to lean forward. Just a fraction. A breath.

But then, I saw something flash across the web. A single word carved in messy handwriting, glittering faintly:

"Fly."

And I remembered something. A birthday card from my grandma when I was eight. She called me "her Skylark." She said I had wings, even if no one else could see them yet. She told me I was born to rise. Not sink.

I jerked my head to the side.

"No," I said, teeth clenched. "I'M NOT YOUR PETTT!"

The collar hissed. Burned. Then vanished into threads of light.

The spider didn't scream. It didn't move.

It *smiled.*

"Oh," it whispered, eyes glinting. "You're still fighting. Good. It'll make the breaking sweeter."

The silk trembled.

The web began to spin again.

And I wasn't alone anymore.

I heard other voices, soft ones. Distant ones.

Breathing from the shadows. *Others.* Were they lost too?

Or had they been *pets* once, just like me?

CHAPTER 4
TANGLED THREADS

The web pulsed around me like a heartbeat, soft, steady, and unyielding. The spider stared at me, a cold, unblinking stare.

Then the world shifted.

Suddenly, I was watching a memory, or maybe a vision. Mom sat alone in the dim kitchen light, the only sound a clock ticking somewhere in the background. Her hair was pulled back in a messy bun, strands falling loose like tangled threads. Gosh, if she would just fix herself up more, maybe my dad wouldn't have left her for Sherry. Sherry's so trendy and fashionable, I hate her. Mom held her phone in her shaking hands, staring at the screen like she was waiting for a lifeline.

I recognized that look, the quiet desperation of someone trying to get it right but never quite reaching the mark. Mom always tried. Always. Even when she stumbled, even when she lost her patience and her voice cracked like glass. She was there, even when she was oblivious.

Her face was etched with exhaustion and worry, but underneath it all, there was something fierce. A stubborn kind of hope that maybe, just maybe, things could get better.

Just then, my dad's voice echoed from some place far away, low, distant, like an echo through a tunnel. He wasn't there. Not really. He left months ago, moving on to a new life, a new family, a baby who wasn't me. I remembered the silence that followed his departure, how the house felt emptier, colder, like it had lost its center.

I saw the last message he sent Mom, short, clipped, without a single word about me. No regrets. No explanations. Just a cold goodbye that felt like a door slamming shut.

The spider's web tightened around my throat, squeezing. "They don't hold you," it hissed, its voice slithering into Mom's gentle tone. "They never held you."

I fought the tears that bubbled up, swallowing them down until they burned my throat. The truth was, they were both broken, mom in her endless struggle to fix things, dad in his escape to a new life. And somehow, I was caught in the middle, tangled in their mess.

But I wasn't just their mistakes. There had to be more than this for me. This sucks!

"I'm not their broken parts," I whispered, voice shaking but defiant. "I'm my own person."

The spider crept closer, legs moving like cold steel, eyes gleaming like polished onyx. Its cruel grin split open the darkness. "But you're still tangled. You're still mine."

I clenched my fists so hard my nails dug into my palms. The silk threads around me pulsed again, tightening, but this time I didn't freeze. I reached deep inside, grabbing onto a flicker of something small and stubborn, a spark of hope, or maybe just plain stubbornness. I don't like your tone and I'm not your pet," I said, voice stronger now. "I'm not trapped. I'm not yours."

The spider recoiled, its hiss vibrating through the web like a warning.

Suddenly, a flood of memories crashed over me, snippets of all the battles I fought inside my own head.

The sharp edge of anxiety, that gnawing fear that made my heart race for no reason. The chaotic highs and crushing lows of mood swings that felt like riding a rollercoaster without a seatbelt. The nights I stayed awake, tangled in thoughts that spun darker and darker, whispering things I never wanted to believe.

The time I hurt myself, scratches on my skin reminded me I was still alive when everything else felt numb. And those darker moments, when the silence screamed louder than my thoughts, and I wondered if anyone would notice if I disappeared.

The spider watched, patient and knowing, like it was just waiting for me to break. Are you supposed to be my friend or my enemy?

CHAPTER 5

THE SPLINTERED WEB

The web was quiet now.

Not still, never still, but quiet, like a forest after a storm. The threads glowed faintly, humming with memory and something else I couldn't name. I wasn't bound as tightly anymore. The silk no longer strangled my chest, but I wasn't free either.

I floated, suspended between what was and what still clung to me.

The spider hadn't spoken in hours, or minutes, or years. Time didn't work here. Sometimes I thought I was still lying on the cold bathroom floor back home. Other times, I wondered if this web was all that was left of me.

I turned my head as far as I could.

The spider sat across from me, watching. Still.

Impossible to read. Its many eyes shimmered like obsidian, each one reflecting a different part of me. Anger. Fear. Guilt. Silence.

I couldn't tell if it was guarding me or hunting me.

"Are you trying to help me?" I asked softly. "Or are you just feeding on me?"

It didn't answer. Not in words. It just tilted its head slightly, like it was curious. Or amused.

Mixed signals.

That's all I ever got, from it, from people, from everything.

A new thread shimmered to life, spiraling out beside me like a film reel.

I didn't want to see it.

But I looked anyway.

A small child, six years old, curled up on a scratchy carpet. Knees pulled up to their chest. Face flushed and silent. The babysitter, older, trusted, was too close. Too quiet. Hands that should've helped to cross the street or reach the cereal box… instead did something painful and unforgivable.

The world spun on, unaware.

The thread pulsed with heat and shame, and I wanted to scream at it to stop, to unravel itself into nothing.

But the spider only watched.

"You didn't stop it," I whispered. I wasn't sure if I

was talking to the spider or myself. "You were there, weren't you? Even back then?"

The spider's legs twitched.

"I screamed without screaming," I said. "And no one heard me."

Another thread sparked beside it, this one flickering between memories.

Mom in the kitchen, hands shaking as she tried to balance the bills, a bag of groceries, and a meltdown I couldn't explain.

Mom yelling, then crying, then holding me like I was already slipping through her fingers.

"You're just like your father," she once spat through gritted teeth, right after he left. "Always running."

But she didn't mean it. Not really. Mom was tired. Always tired.

And he *was* always running.

A new memory spun itself into the silk. Dad's new house. New baby. New Sherry.

Everything smelled like fresh paint and lavender fabric softener. I didn't fit there. Not with my chipped nail polish, my cut-up hoodie, my mismatched energy. Sherry was polite, like a teacher who wanted to be anywhere but at your parent-teacher conference. She gave me side-hugs and fake smiles and the kind of compliments you give strangers at a funeral.

And the baby, God, she was cute.

I hated that she was cute.

I hated that Dad looked at her like she was his *real* beginning.

He barely looked at me at all. They wouldn't even let me hold the freaking baby but instead it was like they were flaunting it in my face saying we got all we need right here and you're not welcome. Like it was loved, and I was just tolerated.

The spider moved suddenly, drawing closer. Its legs clicked softly over the threads. Its voice, if you could call it that, slipped into my head, not harsh, not gentle. Just... *present.*

"I didn't cause the wounds," it said. "I only stitch them together."

"But the stitches still hurt, dumbass," I snapped.

"Yes," it agreed. "But so does healing." Wait What?!

I didn't know whether to cry or scream or beg it to leave me alone. The truth was, I didn't know what I wanted from the spider and what it wanted from me. Sometimes it felt like a demon feeding on my darkest memories. Other times it felt like the only thing that *saw* me, really saw me.

I stared into its eyes, searching for something solid. Something real.

"Are you my enemy?" I asked. "Or... are you the only thing keeping me from falling apart?"

It blinked. And in that blink, I saw a flicker of my

reflection, torn, but not broken. Still suspended, yes. But also still here.

Maybe that was the point.

The spider didn't answer. It didn't need to.

Because for the first time, I wasn't sure either.

CHAPTER 6

WHISPERS IN THE WEB

I thought I was alone in the web. I wasn't.

It started as a whisper. Just one. So faint I almost mistook it for the silk shifting in the stale air.

"Don't talk to it."

The voice came from somewhere behind me, soft, uncertain, like someone who hadn't spoken in a long time.

I twisted my head as far as I could, but the strands held me firm. I couldn't see them, but I could *feel* them. There were others here. Close. Tangled in their own cocoons. Breathing.

"Who are you?" I asked.

Silence. Then another voice, this one clearer. "We don't really go by names anymore. Not in here."

"How long have you been trapped?" I whispered.

A pause.

A breath.

"Too long," said another. "But time doesn't pass the same in the web. It stretches. Like everything else."

I felt my stomach drop.

I wasn't special. I wasn't the only one the spider had wrapped in silk and silence. There were others. How many? I didn't know. But their voices were woven into the threads now, faint vibrations in the dark.

"I thought it was just me," I said, ashamed of how small my voice sounded.

"It always feels that way," said the first one. "That's how it keeps you quiet. Makes you believe your pain is too ugly to be shared."

The spider hadn't moved. Not that I could see. But I *felt* it listening. Watching. Always watching.

"I don't understand," I said. "Is it feeding on us?"

"Sometimes," one whispered. "Sometimes it comforts you, so you'll stay longer. Sometimes it shows you your worst memories until you give up fighting."

"But why?" I asked.

No one answered for a while.

Then, a younger voice, barely more than a whisper: "Because broken people are easier to keep."

The words hung in the air like fog. Heavy. Unavoidable.

I swallowed hard. "But why doesn't it stop us from talking now?"

A slow hum vibrated through the web, low and rumbling, like the beginning of a storm.

"It likes when we talk," someone said. "It makes it easier to mimic our voices later. To twist them."

My breath caught. "You mean… it *becomes* us?"

"Yes," came the reply. "Pieces of us. Woven into its body. Our worst thoughts, our secrets, our shame. That's what it uses to grow."

I went still.

How many pieces of me had I already given it?

Suddenly, the silk around my wrists twitched, as if the spider could hear my thoughts and didn't like them.

"You still believe it can help you, don't you?" asked a voice nearby, sharp but not cruel. "You still think it's your friend."

"I don't know what I freaking think," I snapped.

A pause. This has got to be a nightmare, or maybe I've just gone mad.

"That's how it starts."

I felt anger bubbling in my chest, not just at the spider, but at myself. For almost trusting it. For letting it speak to me like it knew me. For opening up to a freaking spider. It must take a special kind of desperation to do that.

But also, for believing, even for a second, that maybe being its pet would be easier than healing.

"I don't want to be its pet," I said out loud.

The web shook subtly, but enough.

"She said the same thing," someone whispered.

"Who?"

A silence fell over the web like a blanket. Heavy. Cold.

Then, a different voice, older, maybe, said: "A girl before you. Skylark wasn't the first."

The chill deepened.

"What happened to her?"

More silence.

And then:

"She stopped fighting."

I stared into the dark.

And I realized something.

This place wasn't just a trap.

It was a graveyard.

A silken museum of pain and silence and surrender.

But now the voices had returned. Quiet, but awake.

And I wasn't the only one still breathing.

CHAPTER 7

THE THREAD THAT'S MINE

The voices in the web had started to shift.

No longer just echoes of strangers or lost people, I heard her.

My mother. Not yelling. Not crying. But whispering.

"I should have told you the truth sooner..."

The thread pulsed gently by my ear, warm with memory. I held my breath.

"He's not your biological father, Skylark."

My chest tightened.

"I was young. Scared. Alone. When I met him, I thought maybe, maybe he could help me build something safe for you. And at first, he tried. He really did."

The thread shimmered with guilt.

"But when you started to struggle... when your

emotions got bigger, and school got harder, and your moods came crashing down… he started slipping away. Not because of you. Because he didn't know how to stay."

A cold sadness crawled up my spine.

He's not my real dad.

All the years I'd spent trying to be "less", less loud, less weird, less difficult, just so he wouldn't look at me like I was a cracked window he didn't want to fix... and none of it was enough because he was never really mine to lose.

The spider shifted in the corner of my eye. Watching. Feeding on the ache like it was honey.

Mom's voice continued:

"I didn't tell you because I thought it would make things worse. I thought maybe if you believed he was really yours, it would make you feel more… whole."

But it hadn't made me whole.

It made me wrong. Like a mistake nobody knew how to explain.

And yet… her voice trembled with something more than shame.

"But you were never a mistake. You were my beginning."

The silence after my mother's voice faded wasn't empty. It was thick, like the air just before a storm breaks open. The kind of silence that forces you to sit with everything you didn't want to hear.

He's not your real father.

Those words had rewired something in my chest. My heart beat differently now, out of rhythm, heavier. I wasn't angry. Not yet.

First came the confusion. That cold, tilting feeling like when you miss a step on the stairs and your stomach forgets gravity.

I'd spent years breaking myself open just to try and fit into his life, into *our* life. Trying to be less messy. Less wild. Less *me*. All to prove I was enough for a man who was never really mine to begin with.

"I was trying to earn a place I was never given," I said aloud, voice dry like dust. "I thought if I was good enough, he'd love me like he loves that baby."

The web around me tightened and then slackened, like it didn't know how to respond. Even the spider sat still. Watching. Studying. Always watching.

I twisted my fingers inside the loosened silk. My voice came out quieter.

"Did he know I wasn't his?"

A pause. And then the whisper returned, Mom's voice again, but softer now. Exhausted.

"He knew. He said it didn't matter at first. But when

things got hard, when your needs got bigger, he started looking at you like a stranger. And I couldn't stop it."

Tears spilled from my eyes, slow and steady.

I wasn't crying because I was broken.

I was crying because I had been made to feel broken for so long, when I was really just... unclaimed.

Unseen.

And I was tired of it.

The spider moved at last. A slow crawl across the strands. Its legs curled around one of the glowing threads, my mother's, and plucked it like a string on a harp.

"What do you want from me?" I asked.

It didn't answer.

But I felt something shift in my gut.

It wanted me to believe this was all I'd ever be.

The anxious girl. The problem child. The impulsive freak who pushed people away, who lashed out, who couldn't sit still or stay calm or stay quiet.

It wanted me to believe that my story started and ended with rejection. But I wasn't a pet. And I wasn't just their pain. I was *mine*. A girl who had survived a thousand little betrayals. Who screamed when no one listened. Who felt everything too much, too loud, too hard, but *still felt*. And that? That was something worth fighting for. A thread near my chest snapped. Clean. Quiet. The spider froze. "I'm not yours," I whispered.

Not to the spider. Not to him. Not even to the fear that had lived in me like a roommate since I was nine years old. "I'm not anybody's shadow." The silk trembled again, threads loosening like breath finally exhaled.

And somewhere in the web, one of the voices whispered

"That's how it starts."

CHAPTER 8

THE SWEETEST CAGE

The web shimmered again, but this time, it didn't tighten.

It **warmed**.

A strange, thick calm settled over me like fog. My arms were still bound, but the pressure was gentler now, like a hug instead of a straitjacket. Like the spider had taken its many eyes off me and decided to give me space. But I wasn't stupid. I knew what this was. This wasn't freedom. This was sedation. A lullaby spun in silk. "You're tired," came the spider's voice, not sharp this time, not jagged and cruel, but low… almost *kind*. "You've been fighting so long."

I blinked slowly. The air smelled like lavender and something sweeter, maybe honey or jasmine or some scent my brain half-remembered from before everything hurt.

"You don't have to struggle anymore," it said. "Let go. Let the ache settle. Let the thoughts drift away."

It was tempting. God, it was tempting. After all, I was tired. Tired of feeling too much. Tired of holding everything inside so it didn't explode out at the wrong person at the wrong time. Tired of pretending to be okay when my brain kept firing pain signals no one else could see.

Tired of **being the storm**. The spider's silk pulsed around me, warm now. Inviting.

"I can give you peace," it whispered. "No more questions. No more memories. No more messy emotions. Just stillness." I almost believed it. I almost wanted it.

And maybe if this had been a week ago, or even just yesterday, I might've said yes.

But something inside me stirred. A part I hadn't heard from in a while. The part that *noticed things.* The warmth was too perfect. The quiet, too empty. The peace… too silent to be real.

Because **real peace doesn't erase you.** Real peace isn't numb. This was just another trap.

Another method of control dressed up as safety.

"You don't want me to be free," I said quietly. "You just want me *quiet.*"

The spider didn't answer, but the warmth faltered, just for a second. I saw it.

"You want to wrap me so deep in comfort I forget I ever had a voice," I continued, my voice sharpening. "You think if you whisper soft enough, I'll confuse that for care."

Silk shifted across my cheek, like a hand trying to hush me.

"You're not my comfort," I said. "You're a cage made of compliments. You're a lie with sugar on top." The glow around me flickered like a glitch in the dream. I inhaled hard.

"I want to feel again," I said, voice breaking. "Even if it hurts. I want to be loud and messy and *real.* I want the chaos and the confusion and even the freaking heartbreak."

The threads began to unravel faster now. Friction. Resistance. The web didn't like this.

"You can keep your silence," I spat. "You can keep your sweet, empty stillness. I'll take the noise." The spider hissed, not cruel this time, but wounded. And I realized...

I was hurting it. Not with hate. With **clarity.**

Because its power only lived in shadows. In secrets. In soft surrender. And I was waking up.

CHAPTER 9

THE LAST STRAND

The silk around my wrists gave way with a sound like a whisper breaking.

Not a snap. Not a scream. Just... quiet release. For a moment, I floated in nothingness. Limbs weightless. Mind buzzing. My body didn't know what to do without the pressure. It had gotten so used to being held down that it almost forgot how to move.

But then, I moved. Slowly, shakily, I reached out and peeled the last thread from my chest.

I could breathe again. I stumbled forward into the trembling light, away from the spider's nest. Behind me, it hissed and shrank into the shadows, a tangle of legs and unreadable eyes, curling into the silk like a bad memory trying to retreat before being named.

And that's all it ever really was, wasn't it? Fear

without a face. A wound that tried to disguise itself as protection.

But now I saw it for what it was. I was not its pet. I was its *prisoner.*

And now, I was free. But just as I reached the edge of the glowing web, I stopped.

There, suspended in the far corner of the chamber, was another cocoon.

Still. Breathing. Someone was in there. I stepped closer. Threads pulsed around the cocoon like veins, alive, alert, protective.

The web didn't want me near. But I moved anyway. A faint voice echoed from within the threads, not speaking, but humming. A lullaby. Familiar. Broken. It was a child's voice. A girl. Younger than me. Trapped in the spider's version of peace, just like I had been.

And suddenly, it all came flooding back: the first time I spiraled in school and was told to "calm down," the early signs of anxiety brushed off as "just being dramatic," the years of masking, of trying to be less so I wouldn't scare anyone away.

I saw this girl, this cocoon, and knew what it meant. She wasn't just some new victim.

She was me. A version of me that never got out. A version of me that still needed saving.

I reached toward the cocoon, even as the web coiled tighter, hissing, resisting.

"You don't get to keep her," I said. The thread burned my hand, but I didn't pull back.

I placed my palm gently on the cocoon and whispered, "You're not alone anymore."

And something shifted.

Not in the web. In me. I wasn't escaping. I was becoming something else. A survivor. A protector. A voice for the voices still stuck.

The threads trembled beneath me, but they didn't pull me under.

They released us both. And in that quiet, shimmering light, I finally felt something real:

Oh, but wait! There was one more pet that needed my help.

CHAPTER 10

WHERE THE WEB ENDS

I thought it was over when I walked away from the cocoon.

When I freed the younger version of myself.

But the web wasn't done. Because something about that moment, about choosing to reach back instead of just running forward, changed the shape of everything.

The world around me began to twist, slowly, like thread unraveling from a tight knot. The glow dimmed. The silk thinned.

And then I saw them. Three more cocoons.

Suspended in silence, just like I had been. One pulsed with frantic energy beneath its surface, tight and over-extended, like someone trying to keep everything from falling apart.

My mom.

Another was pale and still, faint, distant, like its inhabitant had stopped trying to move a long time ago.

My stepdad.

And the last… it trembled softly like it had always been afraid of waking up.

My biological father.

I froze.

I didn't want to reach again. Not for them. Not for *him.*

But something inside me knew: if I walked away now, I'd always carry the threads. They'd cling to my wrists, whispering what-ifs forever.

So I stepped forward. First to her.

My mother.

Her cocoon hummed with worry, years of sacrifice and silence woven into her prison. The web around her was made of *shoulds, guilt, unspoken things*. Her hands were bound, not by cruelty, but by fear that she had failed me.

"I see you now," I whispered. "You tried." A tear slipped from her sleeping face.

"You were scared and alone. You hid things to protect me. But you *never* stopped trying."

I placed my hand against the silk, and it loosened. The cocoon unraveled gently, like it had only been waiting to be forgiven.

She opened her eyes. We didn't say anything. We just held each other.

And I knew: she wasn't perfect. But neither was I.

We were both just girls caught in different webs, trying to find a way out.

Next came **my stepdad.**

He hadn't been cruel.

But he hadn't fought for me either. His cocoon was quiet, heavy with avoidance. Layers and layers of "not my problem," "not my kid," "too complicated." But deep inside, there was shame. Regret.

I almost turned away. But then I thought of how many times *I* had looked away from my own pain, wishing someone else would handle it.

So I reached out. "I forgive you for not knowing how to love me."

The thread uncoiled, soft and slow. His eyes opened. Tired. Hollow. But no longer closed.

The last cocoon was the hardest.

Him.

My father. The one who didn't want to be burdened with my responsibility. The one who never came back. The one whose silence carved a hole in me so deep I tried to fill it with anything , anger, self-hate, even fantasy.

His cocoon was thick. Wrapped in resentment. Covered in all the things we never said.

"You hurt me the most," I whispered. He didn't respond. "Because you were never there enough to even *try.*"

The web fought me. Tightened. But I pressed my hand to it anyway. "Still… I don't want to carry you anymore. Not like this." The threads hissed, but then they split, slowly, painfully.

His cocoon unraveled. He didn't say anything. What could he have said?

But he looked at me. Like he saw me for the first time.

And just like that, the web began to break away. Not with a rough destruction, but with **release**.

The threads unraveled into strands of light. The air shifted.

I could feel it in my bones:

We were all free. Not perfect. Not fixed. But **released**. From silence. From shame. From being each other's prison.

When I opened my eyes, it wasn't like waking up. It was like **rising from beneath a frozen lake**, light warping above me, sound stretching thin, the surface between two worlds shattering all at once.

The ceiling blinked into existence, not all at once,

but in pieces. Cracks like faded constellations. Dust glittering in sunlight that shouldn't have been there.

My breath caught. The mirror was still fractured. The candle still burned low. The bathroom still smelled like vanilla wax and tired secrets.

But something was **different**.

Me.

I blinked again. My fingers twitched like they were remembering how to exist.

And then, from down the hallway, soft, unsure, fragile as a thread,

"**Skylark?**" Her voice, her sweet voice, my mother, my mommy, calling like she wasn't sure I'd still answer.

And for a second, I didn't move. I let the quiet wrap around me, not like a trap this time, but a choice. Then I stood. Not because everything was fixed. But because I finally knew…

"Hi. My name is Skylark. I'm not broken, and I'm sure as heck not anyone's pet. Who are you?"

THE QUIET AFTER

There's a different kind of silence now. It still visits me at night, curling at the edges of my thoughts. But it no longer claws. It no longer convinces me I'm alone.

I see the world differently. The cracks in the walls don't scare me. They remind me I'm still standing. The noise in my head? I don't always fight it anymore. Sometimes I just listen, then tell it to shut up and move over. Therapy is weird. Healing is weirder. But I'm trying.

I've started writing letters. Not the kind you send. The kind you burn.

I wrote one to the spider and to the babysitter. I even wrote one to myself, the girl I was before the web, the one who thought she had to earn love by bleeding for it.

I even wrote one to him… I didn't burn that one. I'm not sure what to do with it yet.

I keep it in my journal. Next to a pressed feather I found on the sidewalk last week.

A skylark's, I think.

Maybe not. But I like to believe it is.

EPILOGUE - THE THREAD THAT REMAINS

The mirror was still fractured, the cracks like silver rivers frozen mid-flow.

Skylark stood before it, bathed in the faint light filtering through the bathroom window.

Dust hung in the soft, weightless, as if time itself had forgotten to move.

Her reflection blinked back at her. For a moment, she didn't recognize the girl staring through the broken glass.

The one who had faced monsters, who had been one.

The one who had crawled through fear and found herself on the other side.

Her fingers grazed the sink's edge. Cold porcelain. Steady ground. Reality.

But something shimmered—barely there, a whisper of movement along the mirror's edge.

A trick of the light, maybe.

Or maybe not.

Skylark leaned closer. The shards scattered her face into pieces, but somehow, she saw more clearly than before.

The girl she'd been—the scared one, the lost one—still lived in those reflections, tucked behind every fracture.

But now, she could look at her without flinching.

She exhaled, slow and deliberate.

"I made it back," she murmured.

And for the first time, she believed it.

Her chest ached in that tender, rebuilding way—like new wings stretching after a storm.

She turned away for a moment but froze when something brushed her neck.

Soft. Cool. Almost curious.

Her pulse leapt. Fingers trembling, she looked up.

The mirror's surface rippled faintly, as if breathing.

Her eyes adjusted, focusing on the fractured glass—and there it was.

A thin, silken thread coiled loosely around her throat.

It shimmered like moonlight, delicate yet deliberate, resting against her skin like a promising warning.

A remnant of the web she thought she'd escaped.

Her breath hitched.

"No..." she whispered, reaching up.

The thread pulsed beneath her touch, faint and alive, before it began to unravel—slowly—sliding against her skin like a sigh.

She gasped, stumbling back. The last strand dissolved into the air, leaving only the faint scent of something sweet—like rain on metal, or the memory of a dream she couldn't shake.

Her reflection wavered.

For a heartbeat, she swore she saw movement behind the cracks.

A shadow crawling between the shards.

Legs—thin, spindly, almost familiar—reaching outward.

Skylark blinked hard.

Gone.

Only her face stared back. Whole, not yet.

She swallowed and stepped closer again.

Her reflection mirrored her perfectly—until it didn't.

The corners of its mouth curved upward just a second too late.

Her breath caught in her throat.

The light flickered. The candle flame trembled.

And from somewhere behind the mirror, faint but unmistakable, came a sound—soft, rhythmic, patient.

Tap. Tap. Tap.

Like something weaving.

Skylark's eyes widened.

Her fingers twitched at her sides, remembering that other world, that other her.

The sound stopped.

Silence.

Then—just a whisper, so low she almost believed she imagined it:

"Welcome home, Skylark."

Her reflection smiled.

The End

Journal

Journal

Journal

Journal

Journal

Journal

Journal

Journal

Journal

Journal

Journal

Journal

Skylark's Journal:

A Place for You

"Sometimes the scariest webs are the ones
we weave inside ourselves.
This is your space to untangle them."
— Skylark

Facing Your Fears

What does fear look like for you? Write about something that makes your heart race or your thoughts spiral. How does it show up — as a sound, a shadow, a thought, or a feeling?

What would your 'spider' be — the thing that tries to control or scare you? Draw or describe it here.

"Sometimes we name our fear to stop it from whispering."

💭 Inside Your Mind

If your emotions were weather, what would today's sky look like? ☀️ 🌧️ 🌩️ 🌈 Describe why.

____

____

____

____

____

____

What helps you calm your mind when it feels noisy or stormy?

____

____

____

____

____

____

"Even storms pass. Sometimes they leave rainbows behind."

Loneliness & Light

When do you feel most alone, and what helps you feel connected again? Maybe it's music, writing, a friend, or just breathing.

Write about a time when you felt truly seen or understood. What made that moment special?

"Being seen is like sunlight to the soul. Don't hide your light."

Courage & Control

Have you ever taken your power back — even in a small way? What did it feel like?

What does courage mean to you right now?

"Courage isn't loud. Sometimes it's just whispering, 'try again.'"

Becoming

What did Skylark's story teach you about yourself?

Write a letter to your future self. Tell her what you hope she remembers — about strength, fear, and finding herself again.

"I used to think I had to fight my fear to be free. But maybe freedom is learning to look it in the eye and still move forward. You're not alone in the web—you're learning how to climb out."

www.ingramcontent.com/pod-product-compliance
Lightning Source LLC
LaVergne TN
LVHW022013200926
848481LV00007B/2373